W9-BKN-240

EARTH
SCIENCE
PROJECTS
★ for kids ★

A PROJECT GUIDE TO

WIND, WEATHER, AND THE ATMOSPHERE

Marylou Morano Kjelle

Mitchell Lane
PUBLISHERS

P.O. Box 196
Hockessin, Delaware 19707
Visit us on the web: www.mitchelllane.com
Comments? email us: mitchelllane@mitchelllane.com

Mitchell Lane
PUBLISHERS

EARTH SCIENCE PROJECTS for kids

A Project Guide to:
Earthquakes • Earth's Waters
Rocks and Minerals • The Solar System
Volcanoes • **Wind, Weather, and the Atmosphere**

Library of Congress
Cataloging-in-Publication Data

Kjelle, Marylou Morano.
  A project guide to wind, weather, and the atmosphere / Marylou Morano Kjelle.
      p. cm. — (Earth science projects for kids)
  Includes bibliographical references and index.
  ISBN 978-1-58415-869-1 (lib. bd.)
  1. Weather—Experiments—Juvenile literature.
  2. Wind—Experiments—Juvenile literature.
  3. Meteorology—Experiments—Juvenile literature. 4. Science projects—Juvenile literature. I. Title.

  QC981.3.K575 2011
  551.5078—dc22

  2010030899

Printing   1   2   3   4   5   6   7   8   9

                                                    PLB

CONTENTS

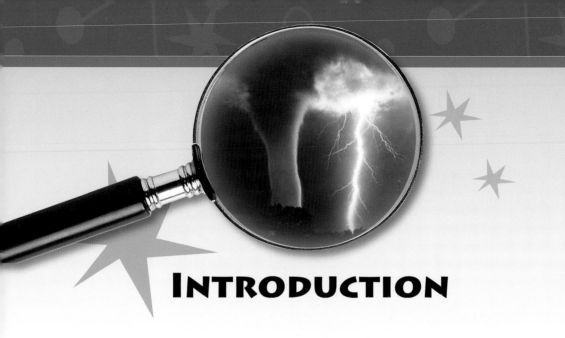

INTRODUCTION

We can't control the weather, but the weather certainly influences us. What we do, where we go, what we wear, and even how we feel all depend on the weather. We now know that weather is caused by changes in the atmosphere—the blanket of air that surrounds Earth and extends skyward for more than 62 miles (100 kilometers). Early humans, however, had no such knowledge. They believed that certain weather, like thunder and lightning, occurred because someone had made the gods angry. Fair weather, on the other hand, was thought to be a reward for pleasing the gods.

Today, weather scientists, called meteorologists, not only understand what causes different weather events, but they can also predict, or tell us ahead of time, what the weather will be for the next several days. They get the information that helps them predict the weather from weather stations, weather balloons, ships, and satellites. Sensitive instruments at each of these locations collect data about the atmosphere. Weather maps are generated from this data, and these are posted on the Internet and shared with newspapers and radio and television stations.

The real force behind all types of weather is the Sun. Even though it is 93 million miles (150 million kilometers) from Earth, enough of its energy reaches the planet, helping life as we know it to thrive. Some of

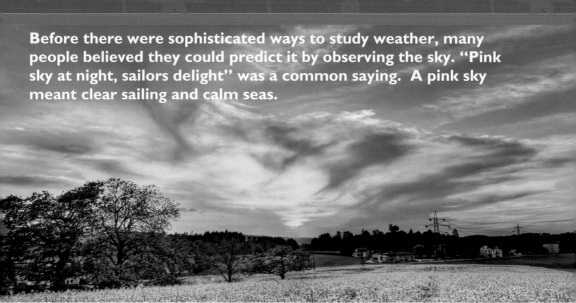

Before there were sophisticated ways to study weather, many people believed they could predict it by observing the sky. "Pink sky at night, sailors delight" was a common saying. A pink sky meant clear sailing and calm seas.

the solar energy that reaches Earth's surface is absorbed by Earth's land and water, and some of it bounces back to the outer layers of the atmosphere. It may escape, or it may bounce right back down to the surface. About 46 percent of the Sun's energy is in the form of light, but an equal amount is felt as heat. This heat influences all of the atmospheric conditions that contribute to weather.

The Sun does not heat Earth's atmosphere evenly. Because Earth is tilted as it moves around the Sun, the equator receives more direct sunlight than any other place on Earth. The North and South Poles receive the Sun's rays at the greatest angle. Because the sunlight is so spread out there, the poles are among the coldest places on Earth. This uneven heating is the basis for the atmospheric changes that produce weather.

Another reason the atmosphere is not heated evenly is that land and water release heat at different rates. Water temperature changes more slowly than land temperature, so air near the ocean is generally cooler in summer and warmer in winter than inland areas. These temperature differences create winds. Beaches, for example, are windy places. During the day, the air over the land is warmer than the air over the ocean. The warm land air rises, creating an area of low pressure. Cooler air from the sea rushes in to take the place of the air that has

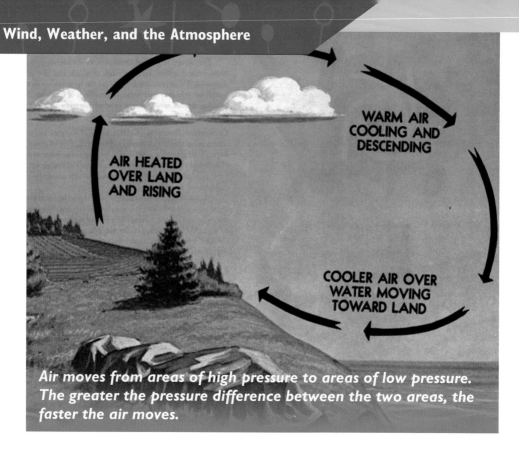

AIR HEATED OVER LAND AND RISING

WARM AIR COOLING AND DESCENDING

COOLER AIR OVER WATER MOVING TOWARD LAND

Air moves from areas of high pressure to areas of low pressure. The greater the pressure difference between the two areas, the faster the air moves.

risen, bringing with it a sea breeze that travels from the water to land. After the sun sets, air over the land cools down faster than the air over the water, and the breeze will blow from the land to the sea.

Local winds depend on the topography of the area in which they are blowing. The Santa Ana winds are found in California's interior. They are felt in late fall and winter and can be hot or cold, depending on where they originate. For example, if these winds start over the Mojave Desert, a desert in California, they will be hot. Hot Santa Ana winds fuel dangerous forest and brush fires.

When the ocean warms or cools unevenly, extreme weather conditions such as floods, droughts, and tropical cyclones are created. One example of this extreme weather is El Niño (The Boy). El Niño is the result of increased surface temperature in the Pacific Ocean. It occurs every two to seven years and can last for up to two years. The effects of this weather pattern are seen and felt worldwide. Not only do weather patterns change, causing more rain and flooding, but people's livelihoods are affected as well. Fish cannot live in warm water. Crops and homes are ruined by excessive rainfall.

There are also times when the Pacific Ocean water temperature is cooler than normal. This is called La Niña (The Girl). The effects of La Niña are often the opposite of El Niño. In the southwestern United States, La Niña produces dry conditions, which ruin crops.

The atmosphere is divided into five layers, but the top three upper layers—the mesosphere, the thermosphere, and the exosphere—are too far from Earth's surface to affect its weather. The stratosphere has some influence over weather, but it is in the troposphere, the layer of atmosphere that is closest to Earth, where most weather occurs.

In the troposphere, four atmospheric conditions interact to produce weather. These are temperature, the measurement of how hot or cold the air is; air pressure (also called atmospheric or barometric pressure), which is the weight of the air pushing down on Earth; wind speed (or wind velocity), which is how fast the wind is blowing; and humidity, or the amount of moisture in the air. These four atmospheric conditions are constantly changing, and whenever one changes, the weather does too. The type of weather a particular place regularly receives is called its climate.

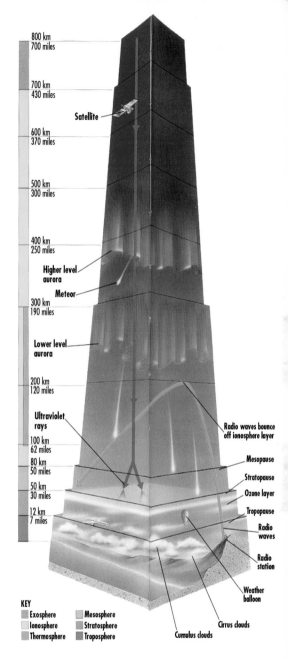

800 km
700 miles

700 km
430 miles

Satellite

600 km
370 miles

500 km
300 miles

400 km
250 miles

Higher level aurora

Meteor

300 km
190 miles

Lower level aurora

200 km
120 miles

Ultraviolet rays

Radio waves bounce off ionosphere layer

100 km
62 miles

80 km
50 miles

Mesopause

50 km
30 miles

Stratopause

Ozone layer

12 km
7 miles

Tropopause

Radio waves

Radio station

Weather balloon

KEY
Exosphere   Mesosphere
Ionosphere   Stratosphere
Thermosphere   Troposphere

Cirrus clouds

Cumulus clouds

Earth's atmosphere is made up of many layers, but only the troposphere is close enough to influence the weather.

The atmosphere consists mostly of nitrogen, but other gases, such as oxygen, carbon dioxide, ozone, and water vapor, are also present in the atmosphere. They protect us from the Sun's harmful rays, but at the same time, they trap and keep heat close to Earth. For this reason, some of these gases are called greenhouse gases. The amount of greenhouse gases is on the rise. Some members of the scientific community believe that a buildup of greenhouse gases is causing the average temperature of Earth to increase, a process called global warming.

As you study the weather, be sure to keep a notebook in which to record your observations and data. Include the date, time, and place of the experiment. Serious scientists always record their

observations in pen. That way, they can go back and check their notes whenever a new question comes up.

Weather is the condition of the atmosphere, and most of the time, it is calm and fairly pleasant. However, please keep these safety issues in mind when studying the weather:

1. Never look directly at the Sun. It can damage your eyes.
2. Never go out in extreme weather conditions, such as lightning storms, tornadoes, hurricanes, flooding, or blizzards. Check out web sites for disaster preparedness, such as the one by the Federal Emergency Management Agency (FEMA) at http://www.fema.gov/kids/. Then discuss emergency weather plans with your parents or guardians.
3. Some thermometers contain mercury, which is a toxic metal. Mercury thermometers are banned in some states. If you have a mercury thermometer, ask your parents to take it to a thermometer exchange location, where they can trade it in for a safer model.
4. Be sure you have an adult's permission before starting any experiment. Please work with an adult for the experiments that ask you to do so.
5. Before starting any experiment, read the directions carefully and assemble all supplies.
6. Apply sunblock if you are working on experiments outside.

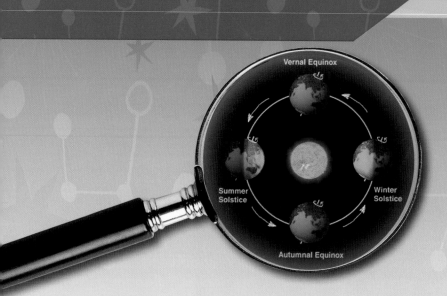

Vernal Equinox

Summer Solstice

Winter Solstice

Autumnal Equinox

THE UNEVEN HEATING OF THE SUN

Seasons are caused by the relationship between Earth and the Sun. Earth is not straight up and down on its orbit around the Sun. Instead, it tilts, or leans slightly. Each of the four seasons has its own weather pattern. Earth orbits the Sun once every 365 days. For some of this time, it is tilted toward the Sun, and for some of the time it is tilted away from it. When the North Pole is tilted toward the Sun (see the diagram above), it is summer in the Northern Hemisphere, and the sun appears higher in the sky. Daylight lasts longer in summer. Air and water temperatures are also warmer in summer because the Sun is beaming its energy directly to Earth.

The Southern Hemisphere enjoys its summer months when the South Pole is tilted toward the Sun. There are also times of the year when neither pole is tilted toward the Sun. When this happens—during spring and fall—both hemispheres receive the same amount of sunlight.

Sunlight reaches various areas of Earth differently. The equator always receives sunlight directly. However, because of the way Earth curves, the North Pole and the South Pole receive sunlight at an angle. This angle decreases the intensity of the Sun's radiation. Because the

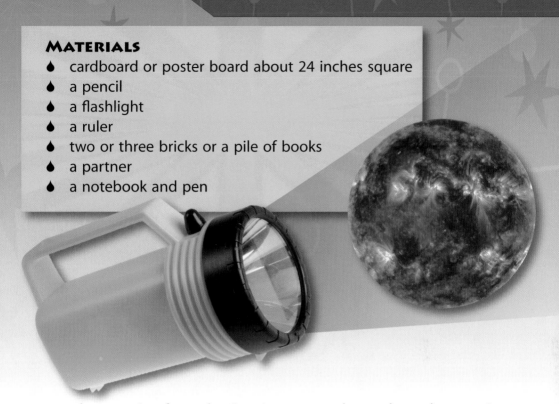

MATERIALS
- cardboard or poster board about 24 inches square
- a pencil
- a flashlight
- a ruler
- two or three bricks or a pile of books
- a partner
- a notebook and pen

energy they receive from the Sun is so spread out, the poles remain colder than other places on Earth.

This experiment will help you understand why the Sun's energy is spread out more in areas that are closer to the poles than in areas that are closer to the equator.

PROCEDURE

1. While your partner holds the cardboard or poster board upright, position the flashlight so that the light shines straight onto its surface. Put the flashlight on the bricks or books to keep it parallel to the floor.
2. With the pencil, lightly trace the circle that the light makes.
3. Tilt the cardboard toward you. Trace the shape the light makes. Using your ruler, measure the length and width of the shape.
4. Tilt the cardboard farther in the same direction. Trace the shape and measure its length and width.
5. Repeat steps 3 and 4, but tilt the cardboard away from you.
6. Record your results in your notebook. Which flashlight position produces the largest shape? Why?

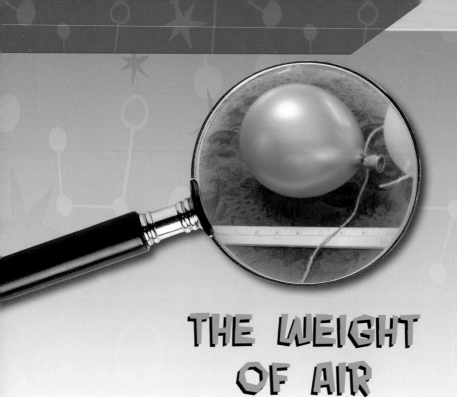

THE WEIGHT OF AIR

It is difficult to imagine that something we can't see can have weight, but invisible air does have weight. To help you understand this, take a piece of chalk and head out to the sidewalk. Draw a square that is one inch on each side. Now picture this one-inch square forming a column that stretches from the sidewalk to the top of the troposphere. If this column of air could be placed on a scale, it would weigh 14.7 pounds (6.7 kilograms). Scientists say the weight of air at sea level is 14.7 pounds per square inch (psi), or 1.0333 kilograms per square centimeter (kg/ cm^2).

You can perform an easy experiment to prove that air does have weight.

MATERIALS
- yardstick or meterstick
- 2 balloons of the same size and shape
- 2 pieces of string, 9 inches each
- sturdy chair
- safety pin

PROCEDURE

1. Blow up the two balloons so that they are the same size.
2. Tie one piece of string to each balloon.
3. Tie one balloon to either side of the yardstick; the balloons should hang down.
4. Place the yardstick with the attached balloons over the back of a chair. Position it so that it is balanced.
5. Using the safety pin, prick one of the balloons. How do you explain what happens?

Both balloons were approximately the same weight, and they both started with about the same amount of air. The air escaped from the balloon you pricked, but there is still air in the intact balloon. The intact balloon weighs more, causing that side of the yardstick to go down. The air in the balloon must have weight.

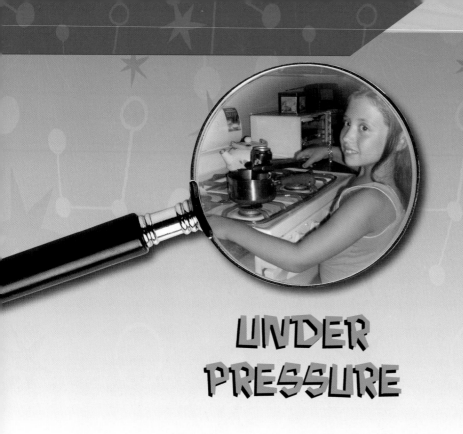

UNDER PRESSURE

Air, like anything else that has weight, exerts a force or pressure on other objects around it. Atmospheric pressure is the weight of air pressing down on people and other objects on Earth. Could you walk around with several thousand pounds on your back? Since the atmosphere is pressing down on you with a force of 14.7 psi (1.0333 kg/cm^2) of your body's surface, you are always carrying that weight and don't even know it! We don't feel atmospheric pressure because the atmosphere is pressing down on us equally on all sides. Our internal organs exert an outward pressure that equals the force of the pressure pushing inward. The two forces balance each other out.

The following experiment shows what can happen when the pressure outside an object does not equal the pressure inside it. **Ask an adult** to help you with this experiment.

MATERIALS

- empty soda can
- small saucepan filled halfway with water
- measuring cup
- stove
- kitchen tongs
- baking pan or dish
- 2 to 3 ice cubes

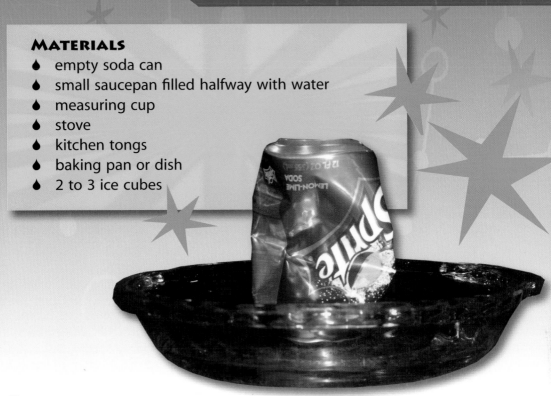

PROCEDURE

1. Using a measuring cup, pour about ⅛ cup of water into an empty soda can.
2. Place a saucepan with water on the stove; turn the burner on low.
3. Set the soda can with the water in the saucepan. Turn up the heat and wait for the water inside the can to boil. You will know it is boiling when you see steam rising from the can.
4. While you are waiting, place an inch of water into a baking pan and add the ice cubes.
5. Once steam rises from the soda can, use kitchen tongs to lift it from the saucepan.
6. Place the can upside down in the pan of cold water. (Be sure the opening of the can is placed under the water.)
7. Observe the can for one minute. What happens?

Placing the hot soda can into the cold water causes the steam inside the can to rapidly cool and condense to water again, which takes up less space. The air pressure outside the can is greater than the pressure inside the can, and it crushes the can.

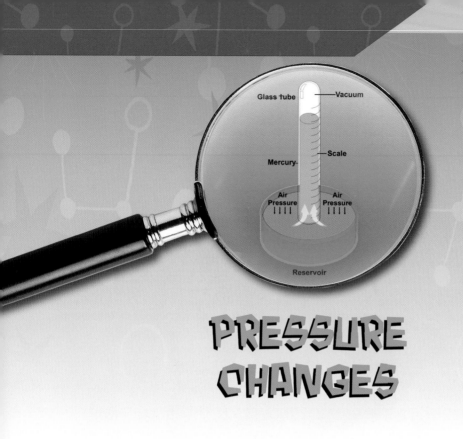

Glass tube — Vacuum

Scale

Mercury

Air Pressure | | | | Air Pressure | | | |

Reservoir

PRESSURE CHANGES

Atmospheric pressure changes with altitude. The higher in the troposphere you go, the thinner the atmosphere. The thinner the atmosphere, the less pressure it exerts.

Atmospheric pressure also changes near Earth's surface. Warm air expands and rises because it is less dense than the cooler air around it. When it rises, it leaves an area of low pressure. Cool, dense air rushes in.

In 1643, Italian scientist Evangelista Torricelli observed that a column of mercury enclosed in a tube rose or fell according to atmospheric pressure. Torricelli's tube was open at the bottom, but sealed on the top. The mercury did not empty out of the tube because there was a vacuum at the top. When atmospheric pressure rose, the column of mercury also rose. When atmospheric pressure fell, the column of mercury fell. Torricelli realized that the atmosphere pressing on the mercury at the bottom of the tube forced the mercury to go higher in the column. The mercury rose or fell until it reached a level where the weight of the column equaled the weight of the atmosphere pressing on it.

Physicist and mathematician Evangelista Torricelli (1608–1647) worked with Italian astronomer Galileo. Although he is best known for his barometer, Torricelli also contributed to the study of calculus and geometry, and he designed early microscopes and telescopes. Physicists honor Torricelli by referring to a unit of pressure as a torr.

This early barometer demonstrated that atmospheric pressure could be measured. The barometers that meteorologists use today are electronically controlled instruments that are connected to computers. In the United States, a barometer measures atmospheric pressure in inches of mercury (inHg). The metric equivalent of this measurement is millibars (mb), with one bar being roughly the atmospheric pressure at sea level.

Changes in air pressure are important because they signal a change in weather. When the barometric pressure is rising, it's safe to make outdoor plans, for clear, fair weather is likely on the way. When it starts to fall, head to the movies. Low pressure brings clouds, rain, and other types of precipitation, depending on the season. On a weather map, areas of high pressure are indicated with the letter H, and areas of low pressure are indicated with the letter L.

You don't need to listen to the weather report or read a weather map to see if atmospheric pressure is rising or falling. You can plan your activities around the weather by making your own mercury-free barometer.

MATERIALS

- round balloon
- jar with a wide mouth (such as a clean peanut butter jar)
- rubber band
- sharpened pencil
- small box (such as a shoe box)
- clear tape
- scissors
- marker
- pen and notebook

PROCEDURE

1. With your hands, pull a balloon in all directions to stretch it. Then cut off the balloon's narrow neck.
2. Stretch what is left of the balloon over the mouth of a jar.
3. Use a rubber band to hold the balloon in place.

4. Tape a pencil to the balloon. Be sure the point of the pencil goes past the side of the jar.
5. Place the jar in a box. Move the jar so that the pencil point touches the inside of the box.
6. Using a marker, draw a line where the pencil rests.
7. Check your barometer at the same times at least twice a day for a week. You will be able to see changes in air pressure by the markings the pencil makes on the box.

The balloon acts like the mercury in Torricelli's tube. When there is a high-pressure system in the area, there will be a lot of air pressing down on the balloon. The middle of the balloon will sink into the jar. This will cause the pencil point to rise. When a low-pressure system comes in, the balloon will inflate, making the point of the pencil fall.

What will you be doing today? Playing outside or staying indoors?

SATURATION AND EVAPORATION

From a sidewalk puddle or dew on early morning grass to rain beating on the roof, water is found in many forms as it travels through the water cycle. Water can be liquid, solid (ice), or gas (water vapor). Sunlight causes the water on Earth's surface to evaporate—change to invisible water vapor. The amount of water vapor in the air is called humidity. Humidity varies according to temperature. Warm air is usually more humid than cooler air. Dry air has little or no humidity, but it can easily pick up moisture in the form of water vapor by passing over a body of water.

A lot of water vapor eventually makes its way to clouds, where it condenses into tiny water droplets. When the clouds become saturated or full of the droplets, they are released into the atmosphere and fall to Earth as rain.

Not all water vapor finds its way to clouds. Sometimes it remains close to the ground as fog.

Dew forms when water vapor condenses on cool surfaces. Dew is often seen on grass in the early morning. When the Sun sets, the temperature of the ground decreases. The warm air cools and is no longer able to hold as much water vapor. The water changes to liquid in the form of dew. The temperature at which dew begins to form is called the dew point. This temperature depends on how humid the air is. Frozen dew is called frost.

You can test saturation and evaporation with the following experiment.

PROCEDURE

1. Place a dry sponge on a plate.
2. Slowly pour ½ cup water onto the sponge until it can't hold any more. This is its saturation point. You may not be able to pour the entire ½ cup onto the sponge. How much water can it hold?
3. Leave the sponge out in the open and check it every two hours.
4. How long does it take for the sponge to become completely dry? How long did it take for all the water to evaporate?

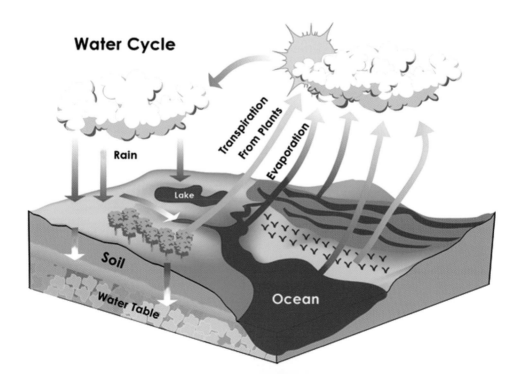

Water Cycle

Rain

Transpiration From Plants

Evaporation

Lake

Soil

Water Table

Ocean

HIGHS AND LOWS

Large bodies of air, or air masses, are distinguished by their temperature, and therefore by their pressure. Air masses that form over the equator are hotter than those that form over the tropics, temperate regions, or poles. Warm air from the equator rises and moves toward the poles. At the same time, colder and heavier air from the poles moves toward the equator.

Air masses sometimes combine to produce a weather event. For example, a continental Arctic air mass that starts out in Alaska will bring cold and frigid temperatures as it travels over the interior of the United States, from the Rocky Mountains to the Plains. A continental tropic air mass that starts out over Mexico and moves north toward the Plains will bring hot temperatures to an area. If this hot air mass stays around long enough, a drought will occur.

You can see for yourself how warm air rises by doing the following experiment. **Ask an adult** to help you.

PROCEDURE
1. Place the thermometer in the cellar or the bottom floor of your home. Wait five minutes and observe and record the air temperature.
2. Go to the next floor of your house or apartment building. Wait five minutes, then observe and record the air temperature at this location.
3. Go to the next floor of your home. (If this is the attic, **ask an adult** to help you.) Wait five minutes, then observe and record the air temperature at this location. What is the temperature difference in degrees between the lowest location and the highest location in your house?

Since warm air rises, the temperature of the air should get warmer as you work your way up to the highest floor of your home. But why should you wait five minutes before checking the temperature on the thermometer?

The United States uses the Fahrenheit (F) scale to measure temperature, but in many countries, temperature is measured in degrees Celsius (C). To convert degrees from Fahrenheit to Celsius, subtract 32 from the F measurement. Divide this number by 1.8 to get the measurement in degrees Celsius. To convert temperature from Celsius to Fahrenheit, multiply the degrees Celsius by 1.8 and then add 32.

FRONT AND CENTER

Air masses are in almost constant motion in the troposphere. A front is the boundary, or line, at the front of an air mass. Fronts are named according to the temperature of the air mass they are leading: a cold front leads a mass of cold air and a warm front leads a mass of warm air. Depending on their positions and movements in the atmosphere, cold and warm fronts can cause a change in weather that ranges from slight to severe.

Warm air is not as heavy as cold air. Therefore, when a warm front meets a cool front, the warm air rises above the cool air. As it travels through the cool air, the warm air also cools, making the water vapor it holds condense. This condensation falls as rain.

Cold fronts generally move faster than warm fronts. Often a cold front will overtake a warm front, creating an occluded front. Occluded fronts also cause precipitation.

Sometimes there is an atmospheric traffic jam, such as when a warm air mass is trying to move north, and a cold air mass is trying to move south. When this happens neither front can move anywhere. Two fronts become a stationary front. They may stay unmoving for days until one

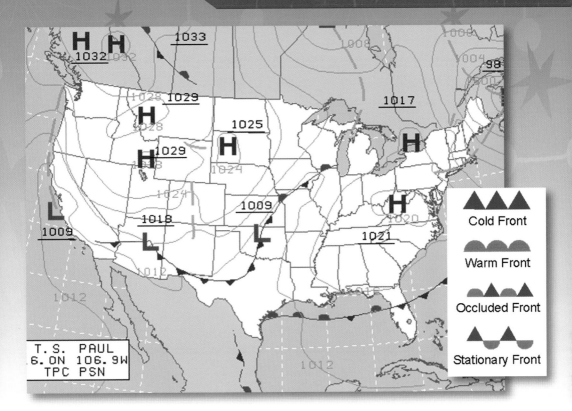

Cold Front

Warm Front

Occluded Front

Stationary Front

T.S. PAUL
6.0N 106.9W
TPC PSN

front gives way to the other. While two fronts are head to head, there will be little change in the weather. People living under the stationary warm front may experience a heat wave, while those under the cold front may experience an extended period of unseasonably cold weather. Once one front finally pushes the other out of the way, the weather will take the form of the front that won.

A weather map is a good tool to use to check out the weather. Different weather events, including cold fronts and warm fronts, are represented by different symbols. A line with blue triangles indicates a cold front. A line with red semicircles indicates a warm front. A line with semicircles on one side and triangles on the other shows a stationary front. A line with semicircles and triangles on the same side is an occluded front. The symbols are on the same side as the direction in which the front is moving.

If you saw the fronts drawn on a local weather map, would you be able to predict the weather?

MATERIALS

♦ local weather map from your newspaper or the Internet (Find a map that is specific to your area. Large weather maps contain too much information that won't apply to where you live.)

♦ calendar

♦ pen or pencil

PROCEDURE

1. Study a weather map, concentrating especially on the symbols for warm, cold, and stationary fronts and the directions the fronts are moving.

2. Based on the symbols you see on the weather map, predict the weather in your area for the next three days.

3. Record your predictions on your calendar, then illustrate them. For example, if you predict a clear day with bright sunshine, you may wish to draw a small sun or perhaps a flower on that day on the calendar. Don't forget to check to see how accurate your predictions are. You can also compare the weather you predict with the weather that is predicted by the radio and television weather reporters.

BLOWING IN THE WIND

When an air mass moves from an area of high pressure to an area of low pressure, wind is produced. The greater the difference in pressure between the two air masses, the faster the air moves. The faster the air moves, the greater the wind speed, or velocity will be.

Around 1805, a British sea captain named Sir Francis Beaufort began developing a system that used the sails of a ship to measure the strength of the wind. The Wind Force Scale he developed is now called the Beaufort scale. Today meteorologists use more sophisticated equipment to measure wind speed, but the Beaufort scale is still used as a frame of reference. At first the Beaufort scale applied only to conditions at sea. Beaufort assigned twelve numerical measurements, ranging from 0 (too calm to sail) to 12 (hurricane-force winds with 45-foot-high waves). Later, Beaufort's Wind Force Scale was adopted for land use. The Beaufort scale for land applies the twelve measurements for wind strength to trees and other objects that blow in the wind, such as flags, leaves, and smoke.

Winds are named for the direction from which they blow, not where they are headed. The directions are the same as those found on a

When he was fifteen, Sir Francis Beaufort (1774–1857) was shipwrecked because a nautical chart contained faulty information. From then on, he was devoted to developing accurate geographic surveys and maps. While a commander for the British Royal Navy, he developed the Wind Force Scale (Beaufort scale) for wind speed.

compass: north, south, east and west. For example, when wind is blowing from the north to the south, we say it is a north wind. Winds that blow between two compass-point directions take the name of both directions. A northeasterly wind comes from the northeast and blows southwest. Wind speed is measured in miles or kilometers per hour on land and in knots on the water. One knot is equal to 1.15 miles (1.85 kilometers) per hour.

Weather reports, especially in areas where cold, northern winds blow, often warn of a wind chill factor. Wind chill is a measure of the combination of temperature and wind. A cold wind will make the temperature feel colder than it really is.

A jet stream is a narrow current of fast winds that moves in the upper atmosphere. Since a jet stream is so fast, it pushes weather systems around the globe. Jet streams also influence air travel. Airliners that are flying in the same direction as the jet stream will reach their destination faster than when they are flying against the jet stream. Two factors form a jet stream. One is the earth's rotation and the other is the temperature of the atmosphere.

You can easily find wind direction by using a windsock or weather vane, but you can't accurately measure wind speed without a sophisticated piece of equipment. You can, however, observe changes in wind speed with an anemometer you can make yourself.

MATERIALS
- sheet of light colored construction paper (8 by 8 inches)
- scissors
- marker
- pencil with a good eraser
- thumbtack
- watch
- pen and notebook

PROCEDURE
1. Make a pinwheel by cutting the construction paper from the corners toward the center.
2. Choose one section of the paper to color with the marker.

3. Gather the corners of the paper to the center and push the thumbtack through them.

4. Push the thumbtack/pinwheel combination into the eraser of a pencil.

5. Take your pinwheel anemometer outside on a windy day.

6. Using the side of the pinwheel you colored with the marker as a starting point, count how many times the anemometer turns in a minute. Record the time of day and number of revolutions the pinwheel made.

7. Repeat the above several times in one day, always recording your results. Is the wind speed strengthening or dying down? At what time of day is the wind the calmest?

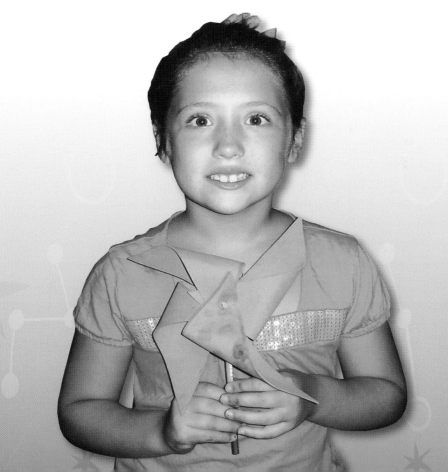

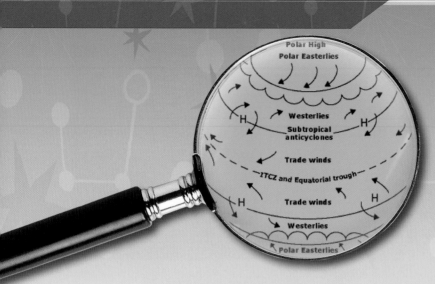

PUTTING A SPIN ON THINGS

Earth is constantly spinning. Looking down on the North Pole, it spins counterclockwise, with the equator spinning much faster than the poles. This uneven spinning causes prevailing winds, also called global winds, to always blow in the same direction with the same force. Global winds are categorized as polar easterlies, the cold, dry winds that blow from the North and South Poles to the equator; prevailing westerlies, the winds that blow from the middle latitudes (23 to 26 degrees both North and South) toward the poles; and trade winds, quieter winds found near the equator.

In 1835, French engineer and mathematician Gaspard-Gustave de Coriolis wanted to find out why global winds followed the same blowing pattern. He studied how unattached objects were affected by Earth's rotation. He observed that objects curved as Earth rotated beneath them. This phenomenon, now called the Coriolis effect, explains how global wind patterns form. You can observe the Coriolis effect for yourself by conducting the following experiment.

MATERIALS

- 12 x 12 inch squares of light cardboard (about the stiffness of poster board)
- 12 x 12 inch square of heavy cardboard (like the side of a packing box)
- nine-inch dinner plate
- metal fastener
- 2 different colored markers
- partner

PROCEDURE

1. Using a dinner plate as a guide, trace and cut out a nine-inch circle on each of the pieces of light cardboard.
2. Carefully push the metal fastener through the center of one of the light cardboard circles.
3. Carefully push the light cardboard circle and fastener through the square of heavy cardboard. Check to be sure the circle can spin on the cardboard.
4. Using a marker, draw a straight line from the center of the circle to the edge of the circle.
5. Have your partner spin the circle clockwise as you use a different colored marker to try to draw another straight line from the center of the circle to the end of the circle.
6. Stop spinning and compare the two lines.
7. Repeat steps 2–6, but this time have your partner spin the circle in a counterclockwise direction.
8. How do the two cardboard circles differ from one another? Which circle represents the Coriolis effect in the Northern Hemisphere? In the Southern Hemisphere?

The line you drew while the cardboard was spinning will be curved. This is what causes global winds. This bending, which is caused by the Coriolis effect, gives us the global wind patterns. These wind patterns always blow to the east in the Northern Hemisphere and to the west in the Southern Hemisphere. Jet streams are also affected by the Coriolis effect.

Cirrocumulus
(mackeral sky)
above 18,000 feet

Cirrus
above 18,000 feet

Cumulonimbus
from near the ground
to above 50,000 feet

Altocumulus
6,000 to 20,000 feet

Altostratus
6,000-20,000 feet

Stratocumulus
below 6,000 feet

Cumulus
below 6,000 feet

Stratus
below 6,000 feet

THE SKY IS FALLING!

As air warms, it gathers moisture. This moisture may form clouds. Clouds are actually billions of tiny water droplets and ice crystals. Not all clouds produce precipitation. Small, white cumulus clouds are called fair weather clouds because they form on sunny days.

Cumulonimbus and nimbostratus clouds produce heavy precipitation, but not all of it makes its way to Earth. Tiny droplets of water are continuously released from clouds, but most of them evaporate before reaching the ground. For noticeable precipitation to form, water droplets must join together to make a drop large enough to last through the long descent through Earth's atmosphere.

Precipitation may be liquid, solid, or a mix of both. Rain, hail, sleet, and snow are all forms of precipitation. Its form depends on the temperature of the air the water droplet passes through on its way to Earth. For example, sleet is freezing rain. Hail is rain that begins to fall and then freezes, but before it can hit the ground, it gets buoyed back up to gather more moisture, and then it freezes again. Layers of ice keep accumulating on the hailstone until it is too heavy to be carried

back up, and then it will finally fall to the ground. Hailstones can be larger than grapefruits.

Some precipitation can be easily measured using a precipitation gauge. You can measure both snow and rain with this device.

PROCEDURE

1. Using clear tape, tape the ruler to the inside of the jar. Make sure the numbers on the ruler are facing you.
2. Place the funnel over the mouth of the jar. The funnel will channel the rainwater into the gauge and keep it from evaporating before you can get an accurate measurement. If you are measuring snow, do not use the funnel.
3. Place your precipitation gauge outside on a day when rain or snow is forecast. Be sure there are no trees, buildings, or other obstacles nearby that will alter the amount of precipitation that falls into your gauge.

4. Watch the weather closely to see what time the precipitation starts. Record this time in your notebook. Also observe and record the time the precipitation ends.

5. After the precipitation stops, check your gauge and record the number of inches you have collected. Then divide that number by the length of the storm in hours. How many inches of precipitation fell per hour? Compare the result you received with the "official" weather report in the news—on the radio, television, or Internet. Did you record the same amount of precipitation as meteorologists reported? How can you account for any difference?

Although it is generally believed that 10 inches of snow has the same amount of water as 1 inch of rain, the National Snow and Ice Data Center reports that this ratio is not true for most of the United States. Snow varies from light and fluffy (when 100 inches of snow equals 1 inch of rain) to wet and dense (when 3 inches of snows equals 1 inch of rain). If you measured snow with your precipitation gauge, let it melt in the jar and measure the water. What was the ratio of inches of snow to inches of water in your experiment?

WHAT IS A BLIZZARD?

A blizzard is a large snowstorm. Three things must take place in order for a blizzard to occur. There must be very heavy snowfall, low temperatures, and winds over 35 miles per hour (56 kilometers per hour). On March 11–12, 1888, Connecticut and Massachusetts received 50 inches of snow during what is known as the Blizzard of '88. During this blizzard, fierce winds caused snow to pile up in drifts that were higher than houses.

STATIC ELECTRICITY

Lightning is the result of static (unmoving) electricity building up in the sky and then flowing suddenly. In storm clouds, water droplets come in contact with each other and exchange electrons. Some of the droplets end up with a positive charge, and some with a negative charge. These charged areas will attract each other, but the atmosphere keeps them from releasing their charges—their electricity is static. Lightning occurs when the charges have built up enough to overcome the resistance in the atmosphere and can suddenly move. Lightning can travel inside a cloud, between two clouds, or between the ground and a cloud.

Lightning can heat the air to around 18,000°F (10,000°C). As the superheated air rapidly expands, it creates a sound wave heard as thunder. You can create tiny streaks of lightning with the following experiment.

FUN FACT: It is easier to see the effect of static electricity in the winter when the air is drier.

PROCEDURE

1. Walk across a carpeted floor. Be sure to drag your feet.
2. Reach for a doorknob.
3. Look carefully as your finger touches the doorknob.

The electrons in the carpet are transferred to you. When you touch the doorknob, the electrons will transfer from you to the knob, causing a spark to appear.

WACKY WEATHER

When they come together in just the right way, air pressure, air temperature, humidity, and wind produce pleasant weather. Unfortunately, some combinations of these four atmospheric conditions can also bring disastrous weather.

Hurricanes are violent storms that form in the tropics. They form when areas of low pressure develop over warm tropic waters. As the air above the water warms and rises, fast-moving wind rushes in to take its place. Eventually the wind and the warm air meet, and the two begin to swirl. If a hurricane forms in the Northern Hemisphere, the wind swirls counterclockwise. If it forms in the Southern Hemisphere, the wind circles clockwise.

As the hurricane moves over the ocean, it continues to draw up moist, warm air, which makes the hurricane stronger and larger. A hurricane will lose strength if it collides with cool air or reaches land.

Hurricanes are known by different names in various parts of the world. In the Western Pacific they are known as typhoons, and in the Indian Ocean they are called cyclones. Winds must be at least 74 mph (119 kilometers per hour) to be considered hurricane force. Most large

Over 1,000 tornadoes occur in the United States each year, although not all of them cause widespread damage.

hurricanes are about 375 miles (600 kilometers) in diameter, but one tropical hurricane, Typhoon Tip, was about 1,350 miles (2,174 kilometers) across. Forming in the Western Pacific in October 1979, Tip had winds gusting as high as 190 mph (306 km/hour) and caused catastrophe in Japan. If placed on a map of the United States, it would cover the western half of the country.

Hurricanes sometimes spin off tornadoes, but tornadoes can form alone. A tornado is a quick and violent storm with a swirling tube of cold and warm air inside a cumulonimbus cloud. Tornado tunnels create powerful vacuums that suck up everything, even buildings and cars, in their paths. They have been known to spin at speeds of over 300 miles per hour (500 kilometers per hour).

Monsoon winds are large-scale sea and land breezes that occur seasonally. They occur on land near the Indian Ocean. In the summer, when warm land air rises, a monsoon blows in a southwesterly direction, drawing air over the ocean toward land. Large rainstorms and violent thunderstorms accompany the winds. The opposite happens in the winter when the ocean is warmer than the land. Then the winds blow

in a northeasterly direction back toward the water. Monsoons differ from ordinary ocean breezes in their size. They can cover thousands of miles (kilometers).

SEVERE WEATHER

SHELTER AREA

MATERIALS

- 2 two-liter plastic soda bottles
- about 2 tablespoons of maple syrup
- aluminum foil
- waterproof tape such as duct tape
- nail
- scissors

Most types of clouds can spawn tornadoes, but cumulus clouds usually don't. However, the one in this picture reportedly dropped a tornado on Watertown, Minnesota, in 2010.

PROCEDURE

1. Fill one bottle halfway with water.
2. Add the maple syrup to the bottle with water.
3. Cut a piece of foil just a bit larger than the neck of the bottle, and cover the neck with the foil.
4. Using the nail, make a hole in the center of the foil.
5. Hold the empty bottle on top of the bottle with the water so that they are positioned neck to neck. Tape them together, wrapping the tape several times around the necks of the bottles.
6. Turn the taped bottles so that the bottle with the water is upside down. Swirl the bottles slightly.

As the water begins to drip through the hole in the aluminum foil, it will form a vortex, similar to one formed by a tornado.

Books

Adams, Simon. *The Best Book of Weather.* New York: Kingfisher Publications, 2001.

Friend, Sandra. *Earth's Wild Winds.* Brookfield, CT: Twenty-First Century Books, 2003.

Maisner, Heather. *Amazing Weather.* London: Andromeda Children's Books, 2006.

Malone, Peter. *Close to the Wind: The Beaufort Scale.* New York: G.P. Putnam's Sons, 2007.

Rogers, Alan, and Angella Streluk. *Forecasting the Weather.* Chicago: Heinemann Library, 2002.

———. *Wind and Air Pressure.* Chicago: Reed Educational & Professional Publishing, 2003.

On the Internet

National Oceanic and Atmospheric Administration's National Weather Service
    http://www.nws.noaa.gov/

National Snow and Ice Data Center
    http://nsidc.org/

NOAA's El Niño Page
    http://www.elnino.noaa.gov/index.html

The Weather Channel Kids
    http://www.theweatherchannelkids.com/

Weather Report for Kids
    http://kidsweatherreport.com/

Weather Wiz Kids
    http://www.weatherwizkids.com/

Works Consulted

Buckley, Bruce, Edward J. Hopkins, and Richard Whitaker. *Weather: A Visual Guide.* Sydney, Australia: Firefly Books, 2004.

Burt, Christopher. *Extreme Weather: A Guide and Record Book.* New York: W. W. Norton & Company, 2004.

Cantrell, Mark. *The Everything Weather Book.* Avon, MA: Adams Media, 2002.

Flannery, Tim. *The Weather Makers: How Man Is Changing the Climate and What It Means for Life on Earth.* New York: Grove Press, 2001.

Ludlum, David M. *The Weather Factor.* Boston: Houghton Mifflin Company, 1984.

Lutgens, Frederick, Edward J. Tarbuck, and Dennis Tasa. *The Atmosphere: An Introduction to Meteorology.* Upper Saddle River New Jersey: Pearson, 2006.

NOAA National Severe Storms Laboratory. "Lightning Basics." Retrieved August 11, 2010. http://www.nssl.noaa.gov/primer/lightning/ltg_basics.html

NOAA's Storm Prediction Center. "The Beaufort Scale." Retrieved September 12, 2009. http://www.spc.noaa.gov/faq/tornado/beaufort.html

NOAA: "National Weather Service Weather Forecast Office." Retrieved August 10, 2010. http://www.crh.noaa.gov/mkx/climate/big.php

Walker, Gabrielle. *An Ocean of Air: Why the Wind Blows and Other Mysteries of the Atmosphere.* Orlando: Harcourt, 2007.

altitude (AL-tih-tood)—Height above sea level.

anemometer (an-uh-MAH-meh-tur)—An instrument that measures wind speed.

climate (KLY-mit)—The overall average weather pattern of a particular place, usually taken over a thirty-year period.

condense (kun-DENTS)—To change a gas into a liquid.

counterclockwise (KOWN-tur-KLOK-wyz)—In the opposite direction of the hands on a clock.

cumulonimbus (kyoo-myoo-loh-NIM-bus)—A cloud that brings a thunderstorm.

equator (ee-KWAY-tur)—An imaginary line around Earth that separates the planet into two hemispheres, northern and southern.

hemisphere (HEH-mus-feer)—Half of a sphere or globe.

humidity (hyoo-MIH-dih-tee)—The amount of water vapor in the air.

meteorologist (mee-tee-ur-AH-luh-jist)—A scientist who studies the weather.

nimbostratus (nim-boh-STRAA-tus)—A dark layered cloud that produces rain or snow.

ozone (OH-zohn)—A gas that absorbs rays of the sun found in the upper regions of the atmosphere.

precipitation (pree-sih-pih-TAY-shun)—Water that falls to the ground in the form of ice, rain, or snow.

saturated (SAT-chur-ay-ted)—Completely wet.

sea level (SEE LEH-vul)—Even with the surface of the ocean.

season (SEE-zun)—A weather pattern that occurs each year at the same time.

solar (SOH-ler)—From the Sun.

temperate (TEM-pret)—Not extreme, such as not extremely warm or extremely cold.

topography (tuh-PAH-gruh-fee)—The shape of the land in a particular area.

tropics (TRAH-piks)—The warm parts of Earth that are on either side of the equator.

vacuum (VAK-yoom)—A space that has no matter.

water cycle (WAH-ter SY-kul)—The constant movement of water from solid or liquid to vapor (gas) and back again.

water vapor (WAH-ter VAY-pur)—The gas state of water.

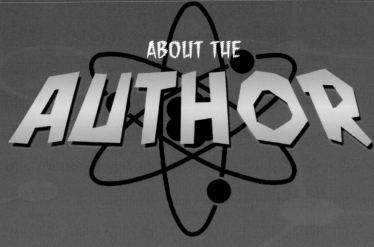

Marylou Morano Kjelle is a freelance writer, photojournalist, and writing instructor who lives and works in central New Jersey. She is the author of dozens of books, many of them written for Mitchell Lane Publishers. She holds an M.S. degree in Science from Rutgers University and has taught science courses to college students. Marylou especially enjoyed creating *A Project Guide to Wind, Weather, and the Atmosphere* because it gave her the chance to conduct the book's experiments with her nephews, Kyle, Ryan, and Zachary, and her niece, Jessica.